THE EVERY DAY

ALSO BY SARAH PLIMPTON

Single Skies

Hurry Along

L'Autre Soleil

THE EVERY DAY

Sarah Plimpton

◊

PLEASURE BOAT STUDIO
New York

The Every Day
by Sarah Plimpton

ISBN 978-1-929355-92-1
Library of Congress Control Number: 2013904314

Design: The Grenfell Press
Cover: Sarah Plimpton, *What Can I Do Now*, aquatint on paper

Some of these poems have appeared in: *Partisan Review*; *The Paris Review*;
Denver Quarterly; *The New York Review of Books*; *L'Ire des Vents*; *Po&sie*;
Le Mâche-laurier; *L'Etrangère*

Pleasure Boat Studio books are available through the following:
SPD (Small Press Distribution) Tel. 800-869-7553, Fax 510-524-0852
Partners/West Tel. 425-227-8486, Fax 425-204-2448
Baker & Taylor 800-775-1100, Fax 800-775-7480
Ingram Tel 615-793-5000, Fax 615-287-5429
Amazon.com and bn.com

and through
PLEASURE BOAT STUDIO: A LITERARY PRESS
www.pleasureboatstudio.com
201 West 89th Street
New York, NY 10024

Contact Jack Estes
Fax: 888-810-5308
Email: pleasboat@nyc.rr.com

FOR BOB

CONTENTS

THE EVERY DAY

twisted into the sky

with your hands

I'd never seen that blue before

wrung out with

the paper walls

of air

until the rain

soaked through

a smaller patch behind the grey

I'd remember once

and then again

like the sun

the every day

THE OTHER SUN

a sudden light

but then you had already gone

the eye is so straight

looking behind

a door to shut

and open

I had forgotten to ask

looking only once

the whole sky

was there

that bright blue

as if painted in

the other sun

EVERY STEP

I would take your voice uphill

in the heat

I had not remembered the sun

something had to break

when you cry again and again

your head against the sky

beaten

in

to light

the night

is just as close

WHEREVER

the eyes narrowing

in the door

round mouths of light

that shut

the air

between the cracks

of blue

small windows

cut in the

winters head

open upside down

the ground

SURFACE

I stumbled

from the height

and fell

against the sky

broken from the edge

the cliff

black against

the stars

falling from underneath

the ground had

disappeared

SMALL HANDS

the mountain shades in the sun

blue

pockets of air

small hands

around the eye

the first green

printed

almost flat

the earth

KNOTS

the light

twisted

in

the head

knotted

behind the eye

its rough edge

catches on the sun

the blue sea of air

BURNT VISION

the night in the head

burning holes

to the sky

stars on the edge

the charred wall

hollowed out

the face

from the sun

SPLIT ROUND

a larger face

the sky

lying open

in the road

split

round at the back

the blue earth

of stones

BURIAL

that bright edge of sky

lined

a solid face

packed in bones

a buried earth

drying flat

on the sheets of stone

EDGES

an eye of broken glass

the sky on its edge

at the top of the wall

the bright line of the day

splintered

from the sun

and already dark

YOUR COLOR

I'd drawn the light into the face

as if quickly

to watch the whole sky once

when I think of color

putting it on here and there

 yours

as if the mountain were yours

fast in the blue

but brighter

the sun

when it is suddenly cold

BLACK FOR WHITE

the black I couldn't see

your hand from the page

outlines the ink

the night

its face

opened in white

a light is broken

in the back

the sharp edge

crosses the eye

the window is on a hinge

turning the night

to the other side

UNDERNEATH

the windows cut

into the road

down to the sky

the earth

from underneath

the night traveling

already shut

catching white

 against

the clouds

THIN EDGE

the day stretched too thin

tearing off

to see

an eye you hadn't closed

the light would disappear

pulled so tight with

the breath

I held too long

shall I go to look

where the broken blue

has turned to

night

TALKING

you talked so fast

I hadn't thought

to walk

and the feet

are always first

carried like children

running so fast

the door is open

green

like the white of the sun

to ask

when I couldn't speak

is it to remember

you had already left

QUESTIONS

I asked again

but it is not what I said

was it the sun that

you made

but the sky has bits of cloud

I'd straighten up with color

working from the blue

the light

to touch

like the air

I talk to listen

like the questions

of a child

you had

already known

ROAD MAP

the sun is straight ahead

I would see to walk

but there is no color

to take out

as bones from

a box

the eye is from the road

and the world is no longer round

BREATH

I opened the door

only once

with an eye to stand behind

the light

driven up

until the sky

was out of sight

the air is cut out

to see

the color black

I was walking so fast

there was

no place

to breathe

BLUE INTRUSION

the eyes

cut through

looking out

such mirrors

of the sky

WALKING

the flowers you like are on the side of the road

a drift of light

is piling up across the eye

my hands are shined again

and again

throwing them out to catch

the air

but I had forgotten that walking

takes such time

and when I looked around

the road had turned

and was

straight uphill

BLUE IN AN INSTANT

where the blue in an instant

lifts the sun

out

I would laugh

catching

catching up

the light

is just behind

from hand to hand

always to remember

the color you said

where the sky is drawn

the face

put down like tears

as white is the half

to cover the ground

AGAIN AND AGAIN

the light is to fold

again and again

packed to remember

the eye

you would know

as if inside out

and all the world

but I will put the color in

like the sky from the sun

as if I never had a name

BOX FOR AN EYE

the smaller sky

from the head

built over

the sun

the clouds

in the blue air

 blocked into light

the eye fastened

into the bone

the earth underneath

DRIFTING

I floated out from the light

holding up as sleep

the dream

so short

from the boat

reaching over

for the stars

down through the water

spots of light

that reflect

in the cold

HOURS TO DAYS

I took the sky by the edge

lifting the color

the red for evening

and drew a line

into the black

a road from the map

yours

to take

the stars are first

with hours to days

did you think I could see

the place for an eye

it is only the night

spread already

face up

with cold

CRACKS IN THE FLOOR

I kicked up the light

as if cracks in the floor

like the earth

walking over and over

to look

where the night has fallen

through

disappeared with its stars

down

the color down

as if the sun

behind the eye

WALL OF STARS

not that I quite want to hold the light

the hands are

built in

and the window broken at the side

the face is from the ground

its dark holes

center

the night in a dark

wall of stars

BURIED FIELDS

the face is broken

open at the sky

and looking in

to see the stars

unwind

the light is down hill

holding to the curve

I run at the road

cutting across

those buried fields

of sight

FORGOTTEN

I had turned around

with every eye

I had thought

I had

the ground had touched the sky

that was where you stepped

in that light

I could remember

but if you talk

it is as if

there isn't the face

and the rain would clear

I had walked too far

forgetting where

the words are underneath

each step

like its muscle

and then they disappear

ONLY NOW

when you can't make the sun

again

to see

the sky put on its

shoulders of blue

the eye is straight ahead

just in front the road

dug up and buried already

the light can be black

and shining

if crows can be golden

my head is outside

its room

its weight

in my hands set down

forgotten

it is the black

I will remember

once

and then again

ATELIER

the light is

thick with paint

I put the sun across the room

picking up the blue

an hour for the cold

when I didn't think to ask

every hour

and then the day

to see

occasionally

a sky

and then the clouds

marked in a

brightness

I hadn't seen

opening the window

you had painted in

SIDEWAYS TO SEE

I walked for the sun

but the breath

breaks

like the step up

sticking to the air

the brightness would burn

away

outside

I stopped to wait

sideways now

across the road

the eye

or none

the cold in and out

laying the head flat

as the sky across the page

for the night

to move

I'll have its light

to color in

CORNFLOWERS

I would hold the face

up to the light

looking through

to the air

a blue haze of flowers

picking up those

pieces of sky

the color of tears

BACKWARDS

which face is taken inside

is it just to see

and not to cry

with eyes like the earth

the cleared air

there are clouds from the rain

the road is so short

and walking to the end

the sun would disappear

the night is from the night before

CLOSE VISION

then what is your face?

I could see the eyes

gathered tight

blue

but then

close vision

is only the air

shining white sheets

of sky

GROUNDED

the door is open

like the night outside

I'll stand to walk

as if the roads

are already paved

but the stars

are underneath

REFRACTION

the blue crack

in the rain

widens through the head

filling

out with sky

drawn at the

edge

an eye

at the line of air

where the light

bends

through the tears

NOW AND THEN

each star is now

and then

I'll count

and every breath

the words can be color

but the eye

has drained its tears

I emptied the rest

even the name

looking out

once more

it wasn't there

the night had no sky

turning inside out the face

to laugh

to roughen the wind

the empty holes

PRESSURE

the sky forced out

with the air

a breath gone

from the dark face

the ground dug up

around the eye

opened and closed

the round hole of light

blackened outside

and squeezed from

the hand

YOU

have you taken

the air

the room is empty

where you sat

the chair is moved to the window

how do you look behind?

is that the door

the sky

has such

light

without

the sun

THE BLUE FACE

the blue face

and the night is off the sky

looking and not to see

the mouth is lying open

only the skin and bone

to touch

the stillness takes the cold

the cross

from the road

STRAIGHT EDGE

the sky held again

the speed

I could run where

your hands had put those bits of blue

along the road

the light will follow

down behind the earth

when the heart is opened inside out

each hour has

its straightened edge of black

PATCHES

I'll put the sky

up to the light

but the sun

is traced in black

and that page

was turned

the night

has its shadows

patched with rain

EDGES ARE STEPS

the curtain has its stars

you wouldn't hear

and the light I lit

has gone

the edges

are steps

with the night instead

OUTSIDE

your window is from the night

are those eyes to see?

and mine?

I hadn't looked

the sky was too close

with its sun at the edge

but the color is black

when you open the face

and the door

is to step outside

WHAT SUN

what sun

so close

to break

the sky

burning off the blue

from the night

behind

the face

the dawn outside

brightening through the holes

strung through the head

the grasses thinner in the wind

pulled in the gate

standing in the shadows

the walls of the sun

PULLING THE FACE OFF THE BONE

you pulled the face

off the bone

holding your arms high

enough

as the night

spreads up

the steps are all the way

to the sky

when I turned to speak

as if the air

had gone

THE SUN IN THE ROAD

is there just the sky

to watch

I'll turn to look for

the sun in the road

but the view is gone

I'll talk again

to hear

the air is tightened

and the light is from there to there

is it where you are

mine is just the heart

and standing up to breathe

your face is broken into light

and the night is on the other side

painted in across the eye

the black sky

holds its stars

like dust

A SHORTENED SKY

a shortened sky

your sun

straight down

cutting edges on the broken light

open up along my eye

the fields inside

laid out flat

transparent

in the air

the head inside a

solid sky

IVORY BLACK

I'll color in the sky

at night

ivory black

made like an eye

to watch

an inside face

a wall of sky

can be cut into stars

but the sun is out of reach

tearing down the road is twice as fast

I could never double back

to see

the day

begin

the paint had dried

before the end

INSIDE OUT

you opened the door

but the face was at the night

you would see the stars

when you turn to leave

the small earth

you dug up

is buried again

tied up in its knot and

the sky was left inside

BLUE ON BLUE

I had taken that sky down

to put away

 clouds and rain

 the sun underneath

as if tears could be undone

the blue is spread on the ground

where you walked

 the cornflowers you said

there and there

picking the sky

 to put in my hand

that day

that one day

as fast as it went

blue on

blue

to choose

BLACK AS IF THE HEIGHT

black as if the height

stands in minutes

looking down to tell the time

over and over

calling the hours

the steps are split like an eye in two

taken down

the white into black

spreading stars

falling away

to make the sky

I would never see

WEATHER

the sun rubbed thin

across the eye

the shadows from the head

straighten into rain

the sky clears behind

empty rooms

of blue

DUSK

the new moon

slips inside

a thin smile

I put the hour up on end

cracked round

your voice that comes apart

AS IF NOTHING COULD BE SAID

you asked a question

about the weather

I'll look outside

and watch the rain

a day goes by

poured out

water from the glass

as if nothing could be said

JUST NOW

the light is to catch

the color

blue like an eye

standing at the door

the sky was only once

and then again

where you walked

the garden has its roses

just in bloom

BLACK PALETTE

I tied the eyes together

and mixed the colors

black

the sun burned through

to see

never seen

enough

the night to paint

and flattened out across the ground

TOMORROW

it cleared

after the rain

the late afternoon

the light

all at once

shining off the leaves

gathered in

untied

I took it

to save

sharpening the face to the wind

not to ask anymore

the light

that was yours

HALF DAY

an hour made up

drawn in black

lines of clouds

folded back and forth

over the sky

staring underneath

the time packed

and sent away

sitting down to wait

STRAIGHT UP

the smile faces up

catching the light

an hour to stop

listening and the wind

changes overhead

the clouds move in

one for another

blind when I looked

and not to the sky

I'd forgotten

to count

WORDS

I was woken up

on the road

lying on words

like stones

at the edge

the whole sky

turned upside down

the clouds are pushing to the side

their same color

has its taste

spoken out

like those words

I would hear

pressed to the hand

and sharpened

to a fist

FIRES

I caught your face on fire

the room too small

to breathe

the too much light

to see

to put it out

as if the sun

and made without

FUSION

a smile to have

made

even as the sky shines

seen

while the sun

burns its wood

from the flame

FIELD FLOWERS

just there

in front

where you spoke

and to wait

the air stands

to one side

flowers in a room

PAINT

I painted out the sky

thickening the paint

white like the sun

covering over

an eye

one then the other

patches of light

to spread

like a smile

AFTERNOON

you made the smile

folded into a small package

put down on the table

to keep

we marched together

there was no wind

only the road

going along

the clouds are like smoke

with the fire behind

SUDDEN WORDS

forced colors

spoken out of turn

flowers in the room

a hand on the door

opened too soon

SPILLED LIGHT

I spilled the light

onto the floor

blinded underfoot

walking away

I held out a hand

black fingers

are stripes

along the wall

DICE

a head shaken

the words like dice

thrown out

stones on the road

to stub your toe

FLARES

you left the color behind

red flowers on the table

holes in the sky

shaped to burn

VISITS

visited

you bent a smile into the mouth

the same smile

muscles in place

forced

as a stick that opens

the teeth

AJAR

I'll laugh

catching on the air

the hands to let go

the breath

and the hours

while the afternoon

is outside

with the sun

spun out

the dark is left open

like the door to leave

A SKY IS DOWN

you sit straight

when the sky is down

black lines of blue cold

drawn

the hours turn your hands

seconds to count

and nothing to remember

OUTSIDE

I took one eye off

then a step

to run out onto the night

breathing inside out

cold air

from the lungs

MASKS

you took out your face

and put it down

the mouth opens

its round circle

black in the air

moving in and out

hung in the center

and suddenly still

BLUE AND BLACK

overtaken

on the road

clouds from behind

pulled along

the wind

blue and black

driven on

DAYS

one day and another

outside

to look

the child jumps in and out

the door

trying the air

the clouds will build

dark blue

pushed under

where the sun splits

an hour off

the words to listen

then to forget

standing still

the earth brought up

to bury the cold

lowering one day

into the next

Sarah Plimpton is a painter and a poet. She divides her time between New York City and France. Her poems and prose have appeared in the *New York Review of Books*, *The Paris Review*, and the *Denver Quarterly* among other magazines. A collection of poems has been translated into French, *L'Autre Soleil*, and published by Le Cormier, Belgium. Her work is in various museum and library collections including the Whitney Museum of American Art, the Museum of Fine Arts, Boston, and the Metropolitan Museum of Art.

How we got our name

…from *Pleasure Boat Studio*, an essay written by Ouyang Xiu, Song Dynasty poet, essayist, and scholar, on the twelfth day of the twelfth month in the renwu year (January 25, 1043):

"I have heard of men of antiquity who fled from the world to distant rivers and lakes and refused to their dying day to return. They must have found some source of pleasure there. If one is not anxious for profit, even at the risk of danger, or is not convicted of a crime and forced to embark, rather, if one has a favorable breeze and gentle seas and is able to rest comfortably on a pillow and mat, sailing several hundred miles in a single day, then is boat travel not enjoyable? Of course, I have no time for such diversions. But since 'pleasure boat' is the designation of boats used for such pastimes, I have now adopted it as the name of my studio. Is there anything wrong with that?"

Translated by Ronald Egan

CPSIA information can be obtained at www.ICGtesting.com
Printed in the USA
BVOW020335020413

317016BV00001B/2/P